T0356018

HELIOTROPIA

HELIOTROPIA

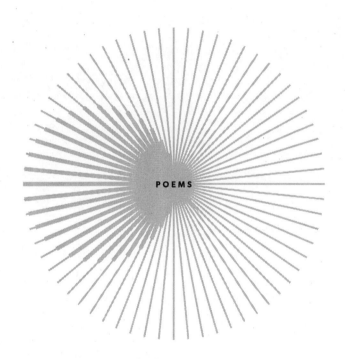

POEMS

MANAHIL BANDUKWALA

BRICK
BOOKS

Library and Archives Canada Cataloguing in Publication
Title: Heliotropia / Manahil Bandukwala.
Names: Bandukwala, Manahil, author.
Description: Text chiefly in English; some text in Urdu and translated from the Urdu.
Identifiers: Canadiana (print) 20240402189 | Canadiana (ebook) 20240402553 |
ISBN 9781771316347 (softcover) | ISBN 9781771316354 (EPUB)
ISBN 9781771316361 (PDF)
Subjects: LCGFT: Poetry.
Classification: LCC PS8603.A6185 H35 2024 | DDC C811/.6—dc23

We gratefully acknowledge the Canada Council for the Arts, the Government of
Canada through the Canada Book Fund, and the Ontario Arts Council and the
Government of Ontario for their support of our publishing program.

Edited by Sonnet L'Abbé.
Author photo by Liam Burke.
The book is set in Plantin MT Pro and Gibson.
Design by Natalie Olsen, Kisscut Design.

487 King St. w.
Kingston, Ontario
K7L 2X7
BRICK BOOKS www.brickbooks.ca

Though much of the work of Brick Books takes place on the ancestral lands of the
Anishinaabeg, Haudenosaunee, Huron-Wendat, and Mississaugas of the Credit
peoples, our editors, authors, and readers from many backgrounds are situated
from coast to coast to coast in Canada on the traditional and unceded territories
of over six hundred nations who have cared for Turtle Island from time immemo-
rial. While living and working on these lands, we are committed to hearing and
returning the rightful imaginative space to the poetries, songs, and stories that
have been untold, under-told, wrongly told, and suppressed through colonization.

for all our tomorrows

C●NTENTS

Season of Sunflowers

I love the sunflowers when they are taller than me
and when they are not. I love the river on a hot

day, when all grime melts into water, and even
when the day is not hot, the river still shuts off

all other voices. I love the sound of the dictionary
read aloud past midnight, not hearing any meaning

but catching bluegrass and verses between the seconds.
I love how precious seconds are, and thirds, and

fourths, and so on. There is rarely pleasure of lasting love
in a first. I love unravelling stitches and unravelling

at the end of a long day that has been full of love or not.
Each day can hold one thing to love, like the love of fresh

red sumac or a hug that lasts, really lasts. The subject
of love is constantly changing, but look, so is my love.

I

Seventeen Months of Distance

August

میری دنیا کے رکھوالے، سن

THE SKETCHES, FROM "MERI DUNIYA"

In this version of the world there is no atmosphere.

Underwater here, we sprout gills along our abdominal walls.

In this version of the world there is no blood.

What surges from artery to capillary
keeping us alive is liquid starlight
distilled each night while this earth turns on.

In this version of the world there is no mercury.

When sick we stretch our hands
towards a sun and read the temperature
in the shadow under our veins.

I would hold you in a world with no atmosphere.

I would love you in the absence of blood.

I would tend the you that leaks out silver shimmer
when you slice your finger turning the page.

July

Some people love loudly!
From the top of their lungs and from the mountain tops!
Some love very quietly, so you have to stop and listen.
There are mountains built of tiny whispers
TOIVO KAARTINEN, FROM FOXES IN LOVE

I have two hands so I can scruff both sides of your beard
at the same time.

I have two hands so I can stop on the sidewalk,
turn to face you, take

your two hands in mine and spin
within the ghosts

of all the loves
that have walked through these streets.

I have two hands so that
in the lingering atmosphere

I can gather the remnants between
our linked hands and squeeze

and squeeze until they sink
into the crease

where your left heartline meets my right.

چاند نے جھک کے کہا
"اور ذرا آہستہ"

FAIZ AHMAD FAIZ, FROM "MANZAR"

My world   an open air courtyard
by a riverbank   built from red brick
from an older century. My world

rolls small into a sphere   I tuck
in your sleeve. There is no measure of time
from the moment   your world
touched mine

to the moment   my heart touched
yours   to the moment I folded myself snug
into the guardian   that is you.

Tonight the river rages
over   the brick. Through
a chasm of distance
fast-filling   with water

I scramble to reach   you.
You scoop   bucket by bucket until
the riverbed only touches my soles.

All we lay bare   the stream carries
away. All that we are
hushes down.   We tuck our spheres
into the guardian   of each other.
All that is left—

the listening   sun
in the courtyard, the brick
where   all breath resides.

May

Marigold Tarot, Partnership Reading

How you see yourself:	*How you see them:*	*How they see you:*	*How they see themself:*
Nine of Wands	Emperor	Knight of Swords,	Ten of Swords
Read in the cards not just who we were before life made us but who we have become when thrust into the orbit of each other.	You, my emperor; I, your path. The cards read not our wants but our needs. The empress is steady in her throne,	looking not for a worshipper but an equal. Your scythe's curved edge sometimes meanders but is always on task.	The wound a knife makes lets out poison and other foreign substances. Blood, after all, replenishes. A love of times past that needs renewal.

Who they are:
Strength

Dill and neem and
other harvests. Hints
of gold ground us to
earthliness. All that
we need, flowing
against wood grain.

Who you are:
Empress

Between both
spreads are so many
knives, some upside
down, the collecting
of life's shambles
into a funnel.

Drop card:
Two of Rings

You reach out your
hand and brush a
finger against my
blade, and I shudder,
and I shudder.

April

*Tell me about the dream where we pull the bodies out of the lake
and dress them in warm clothes again.*
RICHARD SIKEN, FROM "SCHEHERAZADE"

The dream   where our mounts galloped   to the only palace
left standing. The dream   where I caught   a glimpse

of parallel universes and woke   sweating.
          How to tell you   the alternatives

I witnessed? The one where we died old, within minutes
          of each other. The one   where we passed
in a train station once, said *excuse me*   then walked on.

                    A major god
might be able to declare   what universe
          is the best, but us   in our undivine nature
know the best   is what we have. This one

of hundreds of kilometres but also   of three-
hundred and   sixty-five good nights and good
          mornings. This universe where fear   collides

with the little shield   of love. Where love
is semi-dormant but
                    stirring
          awake, steady.

9

March

You want me as much as I want you to tell me
I'm over the threshold
Everything is gonna be totally okay until oblivion
THE NATIONAL, FROM "OBLIVIONS"

Do not say the word *love* standing inside the love room.

February

after Lovers, *by Egon Schiele*

I could trace my own outline
uneven

so you might approach me,
head hung over, asking. Or
you might not ask.

You may rest your chin
on my thighs, arms
folded over, both our eyes
closed. I may hang my head

lower so all my split ends brush
your forehead, the travelling
of grief from strand

to strand. Not every moment
has to hang framed
in red and pink.

We stay as lines, paper
on a desk by the window,
corners fluttering
for the better part of a year.

January

No step we make moves celestial bodies, no touch
leaves a room dripping with sweat and salt.
We are not entrusted with anything so grand

it would shift the distance of earth to sun.
Only with each other, to slip away from the chaos of being
to where love is always within reach.

December

You know, in seventeen days, in the northern hemisphere, the days
will begin to get longer again (I know you know this but thought
you could use the reminder)
RAHIM LADHA, @RMNARRATIVE

The moon is a curl of lily of the valley.
Wolves sing hour-long songs

when called upon to howl.
The sun is hammered-down fragments

of turquoise and jasper. Where water
flows into the mountain,

lick sweet algae off the cave wall, no
rose syrup could compare.

I left bouquets to dry from stalactites
and now we tiptoe, careful

to not disturb the petals or any new
seeds they may carry. Life is always

blossoming somewhere. See,
cave ice, new saplings. If they can bide

their time till the sun films through
the cave again, so will we. Take

the lengthening nights for what
they bring, all the more time to hold

the very heart of you that, like
the mountain ridge, needs not be redrawn.

November

میں راستہ ہوں، ہر جگہ ہوں، لاپتہ ہوں

MEESHA SHAFI, FROM "MEIN"

Our words spill
onto the steps
in a slow film of ice

sculpting the breath
of all words yet to be said.

I pick up the art piece
and take it home,
hang it above the front door,

a small du'a
to the bigger du'as.

The soul loses its calloused edge
walking hundreds of miles
barefoot
after Ashura

becomes the path becomes
the place becomes as untraceable

as each word said
before we met.

October

I fear the you that appears to me when I sleep.
There is always blood, a talon or antler. Deer
are carnivorous. One of us lies still beneath
the predator's hide, urging the other to run
with a last breath. The you that is awake
mails me a blade. I tuck it in my pillowcase.
I meet you in the same dream where we stand
back to back, weapons unsheathed. Near the end
of the night we lie back beside the bloody mess
of feathers and hooves, looking up at the sky,
playing I-spy with the crescent moon.

September

میں پیلی سحر کا نشہ ہوں

PRATEEK KUHAD, FROM "SAANSEIN"

We lie on our backs,
two otters waking from a long, long sleep.

August

But I remember your knowing,
your fear. How you held me like we hold the things we lose.
MATHEW HENDERSON, FROM "PRINCESS MONONOKE"

I dig out a hole and find things I once held
so tight, though nothing stopped their time to leave.
Fur shed when they moved

into bigger and better lives. We are never ready
to absorb the emptiness of loss, but must

pause to howl at the chameleon of being. The closer
I prowl, the tighter you hold, the deeper a growl.
My wolf is only just learning

the antonym for starvation. I know
you have your own wolf running circles
in its cage. The circle is slow-growing, but
it is growing. I am, and you are, growing.

July

In another life, I would have really liked just doing laundry and taxes with you.
WAYMOND WANG, IN *EVERYTHING EVERYWHERE ALL AT ONCE*

I do not want to be the first to say good night

but if I don't say good
night now I'll spend
all night telling you

about the dog
playing frisbee at the park. It was fluffy
and bad at catching.

Before we sleep:

[new photo] my spider plant resting just outside the sun

                              can we name it for the sky?
the sky that carries our sun

                    [new photo] the cat jumped on my lap and she agrees
where will you find your joy tomorrow?

                         [new video] tomorrow I will play you this song

I find love poems
bursting
from my texts:

[new photo] breakfast today was scrambled eggs and chili

                         three dragonflies hovered around me in the park
here is a poem I would like to read you tonight

                         [emoji of a sun setting over a city skyline]
settle between my legs and rest your head over my heart

                              I would like to hear your body read

June

I think we are like the pages
of a love letter written thirty years ago
that some aging god still reads each day
ELLEN BASS, FROM "GETTING INTO BED ON A DECEMBER NIGHT"

I archive my longings with botany. I archive them
with poems that become smoke. Take

this jumbled bouquet: irises, goldenrod,
hyacinths, all crawling with ants and other unnamed

bugs. A bleeding heart could lie cleaved
on the sidewalk, its two halves

only millimetres apart, all that is left
an archive of sadness. But that is not our future,

and that was not our path. Our tomorrows
preserve a love that will come. The archive

is now a greenhouse, lush from the seeds of early meeting.
A meeting that was not yet love, not quite absence.

The burying of seeds in autumn before frost.

May

I am a real bear   with a head full of hazard and light
HEATHER CHRISTLE, FROM "JE M'APPELLE IVAN"

Guitarists have   their own graveyard   at the edge of the
courtyard. In the bustling day   there is only a faint hum.
     At night,   the still night   when beloveds   have retreated
to their rooms,   face outwards to the desert   perch on the
swing. The gentle *creak creak creak*   blends with the
chord progression   of an afterlife in the wind   a kingdom of
     animal light   where each growl   is a riff. The refrain an
illusion   of aloneness   in an atmosphere   comprised of
     all that was once   corporeal. A dog now gone   barks a
melody   with the strum. Each swing   is a string
reverberating in the hollow   courtyard. Do not   say the
word   *haunting* in the graveyard   of guitarists; it is life
that carries the melancholy of being.

April

I crawl to a bench
in a forest of tears
on the day raindrops
crystallize. Hold out
my palm, not knowing

if the tickle up my pinky is
the beloved
I wait for

or a nest of spiders
spinning lonely webs
above the bare branches.

A fire hovers
above the treeline, far
from the scrub. Mist surges
upwards in a flood to form

a mirror
reflecting back
your now-presence

in the forest, the self
I swam through fog to reach.

II

1996

I wasn't born yet. Not even conceived.
Five hundred years later in the 24th century,
starship captains will travel millions of light years
in search of humanity's specialness.
As though there is not enough love on Earth.
One day we'll chase the stars. As though
there is not enough war. The earth wars back
with consequence: melted ice cream,
an unfrozen lake, a layer of ice on the driveway.
I step into the river despite my toes already
feeling the chill, despite knowing my path
is tenuous at best. Survival instinct kicks in
at the strangest times. The world has so many
ghosts, all leaving footprints of regret.
When I write I regret that I am not sleeping.
When I wake from a dream struggling to keep
the details of the riverbed, I regret forgetting.
One day I'll be a ghost, lingering outside
all the places I didn't get to see. A baby
might be born the same day I die, another
person on the list of people I'll never get
to meet. I would like to go back,
to when I wasn't yet a body, when I was barely
an idea. To know, in retrospect, the serenity of
non-existence. To float down the river's old
path before the sand pushed it five kilometres
west, before I'm left hovering in the oxbow
without a current. I see the dead and those
not yet born. And when I'm finally born
I'll know my regrets. I won't change
a single one. I'll roll down the stairs
at six months old, my first unrecalled brush
with an ending that never was. At three years,
I'll wade into a lake, bubbles
surfacing, until someone walks by
and yanks me out.

The Splitting

It wasn't until Gabriel squeezed away what was empty in him that the Prophet could be filled with miracle.
KAVEH AKBAR, FROM "THE MIRACLE"

Makkah, 622 C.E.

Inside a house built over packed dirt
from pillars of date palms and sun-dried sand,

the illiterate man
                              unable to fall asleep.

The sound of his camel shifting its weight
from right leg   to left

could be the closing in of enemy men. He squeezes
his eyes shut,
                              his body in
on itself.

•

The illiterate man feels
     in the dark   for words
he did not write.

Outside his house, some men say
he is a madman, others say he is
a poet

who believes enough words will build a bridge to a life after now
where only beings lighter than air float.

But the illiterate man is neither. Palms on the sandy ground, he recites,
SAY: I SEEK REFUGE IN THE LORD OF DAYBREAK.
Each word is a brick

pressed into the thin walls. The camel, drowned out.
The enemies. The screams
stirring within.

•

The illiterate man's elusive promise of afterlife. The now. A split
between seeing eyes by day and sniffing out magic by night.

Outside the illiterate man's house,   a chanting.
Mischief of darkness. Mischief of magic. A split
between silent   and cavernous.

.

•

Magic is not real. Magic takes hold.

•

The best way to kill is with a
         knife. The   best way to kill is
      with a sword   . The best way
      to kill is   the one that is
         successful.   The way that
involves words.

•

30

The wind is a carrier of words. Words of conspiracy, floating
through the men circled around their enemy's house.

Inside, the illiterate man recites, SAY: I SEEK REFUGE
IN THE LORD OF MANKIND, casting a ward of protection

as he rides out through the city on sand waves
in the pre-dawn breeze. There is no fear
of being caught. Who is there   to catch?

Outside the men stand around and argue
the best way   for as long as is left
before night splits.

•

Daybreak   is a slow creep.
Soon all   who sleep
who chant   who lie awake
between calm and panic
will split.   The last night
in this city   where words
are swords   to the one where
words become wards.

•

Still not a madman nor a poet. Still a man. On the verge of a split.

.

Daybreak. The wind lifts. Most words
disappear.
          The illiterate man's camel
sits outside, spitting onto the now-brick walls
of the empty house.

Threshold Ghazal

There's a home on the other side of the world becoming a house.

My memories are here: the ribbon of a prom corsage
tied in a tight bow, ink-blotched letters in Urdu from a friend

I no longer text, fading photographs of people
who have left houses behind too, making homes somewhere

I won't ever enter. My grandparents are making their home
somewhere I won't ever enter, in a room woven

with old saris and lined with books in languages I haven't
learned to read. I know so much less. The sari room

has a threshold impossible to cross. A border is made up
of more than checkpoints and guns. When I book

my flight to a place without a home, a text message
pings, reads: *avail. credit balance is below threshold amt.*

A doorway only reminds me what I can't cross.

•

Summer is eleven months long in my lifetime,

brings too much water and not enough. Staying put here,
where turkey tails sprout over logs through snow, is less

of a choice. I drape a sari from memory and don't move
for hours. When I do take a step forward the silk

unravels. The garment and I know each second we had
was a miracle in itself, a prayer I wasted sitting in the dark.

When it sits pleated in place the pallu is another border
under a winter coat for a fabric that never knew cold.

Cold is what a home becomes when it starts turning
into a house. All the ants leave carrying an old word,

the last food crumbs, out. Crows move in, cawing
the old ghazal. Somewhere, a border is a desire

to flank the doorway, echo the last word.

•

A ghazal is anything music enough to wall against

forgetting. A song or a line on repeat above the buzz
of another language. I flatten the corsage in my palm

under the touch of floral linger. There's a place full
of books I have read in languages impossible to forget.

Forgetting is possible to recall, especially the first word
I ever heard. It's easy enough to make up memories

years from now in a twelve-month summer as I trudge over
endless mushrooms peering through moss. Walking costs less

than flying. I try bargaining with the crows but they say
their murder is different here, so I settle for an hour

of silence in which I can listen to the way a ghazal
invites a single word through the threshold.

I stay outside, hammering the word to the outer brick.

After Winter

When all this snow melts

I will lie in a park, legs

itching from wildflowers.

I will read this poem to

the sun and the sun will listen.

Perhaps you will also be here,

lying in this park, listening.

Love Language

Even at its most difficult
love is worth loving.

I am falling in love with
the change from crown molding to creeping

plants. With improperly pressed irises
rotting purple ink in my sketchbook.

Every rock becomes heart-shaped
when I squint. Clay pots wash up

on the riverbank, fully intact. I am falling like
falling is really flying is really swimming

across the water blackened with night. Every day
I practice being alive. Try to fall

in love with something new. Gold paint flecks
on the popcorn ceiling. Hogweed. I too

am poisonous to touch. Gujarati is not a love
language, but I fall in love with how home

is not home without it. Fairy lights
strung across balcony windows

though half the bulbs are fused. That empty
stretch of riverbank, now that the tide

has crawled away, but something else
will hold that space. Sun to air,

ducklings to the rocks; me, leaning into love.

III

I over hand over

I surrender an unpeeled clementine bursting with seeds

I surrender an afternoon to the lengthening shadows of summer pines

I surrender my thighs burning against the uphill slope of Tenth Line West

I meet my friend in the park

•

In the grass with our bikes lying between us, we read aloud the words of Noor Naga's *Washes, Prays* to still air

"I do not want to love you in an imaginary place"

•

sur (over) + rendre (hand over)

I over hand over

•

I loved him the way I wanted to love the earth. My nose pressed into freshly dug garden soil. Small buds appeared on the rose bush. Last year's thorns pricked my cheeks. He did not lick the blood clean from my face. I wanted to love him while loving my sisters and mother and laundered sheets and pots of snake plants. Ants looped bangles around my broken wrists. Scar extending from my left pinky to protruding bone

•

(v): to yield, the decision of

(n): an instance of surrendering

•

How easy it was to fall into a state of tallying cruelties on the fridge. I did not open the fridge to take the fresh spinach. It wilted, sitting next to the carton of spoiled milk. The way I wanted to forgive. Surrender as an instance of hurting. He said love could have worked. But what of the way the sky does not have a colour? So many words never found their place in the air. So many green raspberries on the bush, half-chewed and hardened

•

My friend poses a question from Bhanu Kapil's *The Vertical Interrogation of Strangers*

"What are the consequences of silence?"

•

forgive = give up

i.e. not forgiving him but relearning handing over

i.e. I give over to the softness of July's ripening fruit

i.e. myself, the grass, summer pollen

•

I forgive the earth through pressed irises that dry translucent. Skin heals over my bones though they still ache sometimes. Lily of the valley, I of the fountain. The places I belong bloom open. A body does not have a single shape, but there is shape for all of them in here. Forgiving myself is ongoing

•

I try not to be at war with memories

I teach myself that I can be my own divine agent

I practice surrender in the name of something I believe in

•

Before I bike back to curl in for the night and recount the day's creaking swing-sets to you. A last poem before the sun sets on a summer picnic, Nicole Sealey's "Object Permanence"

"There's a name for the animal

love makes of us"

•

*dō- = Proto-Indo-European root meaning "to give"

•

To you I would hand over all my roses and spider plants. Giving is easy. I read you a poem in the thunderstorm by lamplight. I read with your breath sighing into my body. In Urdu when I say yesterday I could mean tomorrow. Kal is kal. Because I know that yesterday I pressed your fingers into the dips between my ribcage; tomorrow, I do not need to know

•

In bed the creases of my sheets fit around the creases of my calves my pillow hardens against the flat of my back hand looped through bedframe I surrender to a soft glow

•

I have so much love to give. Yellow flowers in August. Clay mug carved with a village. Money plant twined around banister. You do not need to take anything. I hand all over

Walking through rainstorms

I hold you the way astronomers
draw constellations for each other
in the markets of wisdom
MICHAEL ONDAATJE, FROM "THE NINE SENTIMENTS"

I hold you the way sandalwood embers ash onto a white desk after
the air has cradled burning incense for nine sunrises   I hold
you the way garden trees suck up fertilizer from flower beds bursting
their red berries onto empty beer cans   I hold you the way
astrologers read the minutiae of our joys (the intricacies of our grief)
in the mirrored curves of our jawlines   I hold you in carved
mountain caves where we lie down and let the jungle vines squeeze
around our joined wrists   I hold you the way a ladybird once
tickled its way down my index finger (skim a hand along your spine
(look at you looking at me like the touch of my toe to your shin is
like being held so tight you cannot breathe))   I hold you the
way light refracts saffron off your sweaty forehead as I ride you to
orgasm   I hold you the way old palace turrets invite birds to
gather at midnight on the sleeping island   I hold the grief that
roots in you and you hold mine (grief does not uproot when held but
we hold it anyways)   I hold your hand against my butterflies
on summer walks pressing my palm against yours when my fingers
ache (they ache from the act but never from the intent (the intent of
holding is nine postcards of places where I will hold you one day))
I hold your face to my chest when morning dew sniffs out lingering
sweat   I hold your ear closed with my collarbone as if to say
the world no longer is (the world always is but in the brief moment of
my skin against your skin it is not)   I hold your body with my
heels crossed over tucked snug in the small of your back my whole
heart untranslated   I hold you

Jet Lag

The day before
I came home
you replaced
all the curtains
and painted
a thousand tiny dots
on the ceiling.
When the wall clock
ticks to nine, you
lower down
blackout curtains
and a thousand
tiny stars twinkle.
You promise
to kiss me at ten.
At ten, you kiss
my head. I've fallen
asleep and don't
register the kiss.
I wake up at four
in the morning
thinking I'll get
a head start on
unpacking two weeks
of my life. But
my suitcase is empty;
dirty clothes are
in the hamper,
clean ones hung up.
You sniffed each
shirt to determine
which were worn.

You hung up my
earrings, sorted by
size and colour, hooks
all pointing the same
direction. There's
nothing left to clean
so I come back
to bed and kiss you.
You don't wake
but you stir, emit
a hum, rotating away.
You tell me you know
I'm here now
from the way
your back is naked
and open towards me.

Archive of love in botany

Aster and solidago

Aster and goldenrod take off in a greenhouse to another sun
far, far away. Spring's lost hour emerges
where purple and yellow
take stock of golden days to say,

Yes, I will bloom alongside you season
after season. Our love is like that,
a space opera where most days
we say,   *My brain isn't*

all here today. Goldenrod, a hundred places at once.
Aster, reliably there when goldenrod
collapses in despair.

Bougainvillea

Bougainvillea, paper-thin pink, presses into the paper
on which we pen a hundred hearts

in lieu of promises:
I promise each day
will bring a new kind of flower. A new sun
is on its way to replace our own as it verges
on burnout. Tomorrow will have no break-up
poems. There will always be someone who loves you.

We stain the page until it tears.
There are more love poems to write.

Dicentra canadensis

Bleeding hearts are always break-up poems,
a love poem in their own way.

We have each cried on our street corners
next to bushels of bleeding hearts   blooming
and breaking.

                    We love, despite,
collecting the litter of split hearts. Each poem is a patient
love letter   that knows it will be
reread.

Helianthus annuus

Sunflowers dot planters outside the library;
                              each a love poem
for a love that shelters you.

In a sunflower's disk spin a hundred florets, love poems
within poems. Ray flowers fall
                              outwards and down
onto the parking lot asphalt. Every day

is a new reason to gather fallen petals and arrange them
on the kitchen island. To be marvelous enough

for the sun, the first to capture a new day's light.
Neither ray
                    nor disk compete. Combined,
a halo for the bee; for you, for me.

Jasminum

Jasmine, a scent-guided poem to sieve nostalgia.

Do not ingest, do not approach. Regard this poem
from the other side of the sidewalk.
                                    Some words
appear best under a petal moon.

On clear sky nights I invite you for a stroll. Our words
are floral stain on the dark road. We glance up

to the sky for an invitation lost on a day
when no flower   was poem enough.

Lilium lancifolium

Tiger lily shrivels inwards every summer night. Yet walking
the same path at noon
                        its orange petals are reaching
again. I reach for you

across the sunflower planters and jasmine trees. Our shoes
crush fallen pink petals and pistils.
                                    Above us a spaceship
travels, yellow and purple sprinkling
out of its hull.

To the aster and goldenrod, watching with the sun's
orange glare behind, we're just two black specks

standing on an earth long left behind.

Watching *Star Trek* with you

after The Next Generation, *Season 2, Episode 20: "The Emissary"*

Haven't you heard the first rule, Worf?
You never say *I love you* on the first date.
Or at least, you never ask for
forever after the first mate. We're all here

circling through one planetary orbit
to another, just trying to find our own place
in the farthest ends of ever-infinite worlds.
We know, you'd say, "tlhIngan jIH"

—but there's something holographic in all of us
that flickers as blood drips down
from her palm to your arm. We get the impulse.
When skin is to skin a pulsar, we too would tilt

our heads up to the sky and harmonize with a
growl. We'd want her to stay. To slay
our enemies and then draw our blades
at the other's throat before we growl. Haven't

you heard, Worf? Of the slow game: love
poetry's fullest flowering in the great expanse
of untrekked space. So human
is trust, we inevitably orbit back around.

Before Clarity

I am you in your jewel-domed reading room,
I am you in your kayak skimming.
PHYLLIS WEBB, FROM "THE AUTHORS ARE IN ETERNITY"

The sky is inverted. I call you in the bare yellow night.

I am you against the river of clouds,
I am you in an energy-current trembling down the bedroom walls,

you in the contrapuntal stream of two trees
racing vertically away from the earth.

The sea is inverted. Midnight sun
at our southern latitude glows beneath our feet.
I call you from the land that is now our sea.

There is no becoming; I always was.

Now all events are kisses, a softness
in the morning before clarity settles in.

You in the exhalations that clear out the day's old dust,
you, large enough to hold the sun.

The vapour of knowing might be lost, the dream
we never woke from. You,

I am floating in salt water in our sea that was once land.

Spring, as witnessed

by the cardinals:

I was alive yesterday; where were you? Preparing to take our last walk, to become the season the cardinals settle into.

by the lilacs:

The lilacs want to tell you something. I tuck a sprig behind your ear so you won't miss a word.

by the shadows:

An astrolabe, all its dials pointing out the movement of the sun, flowers.

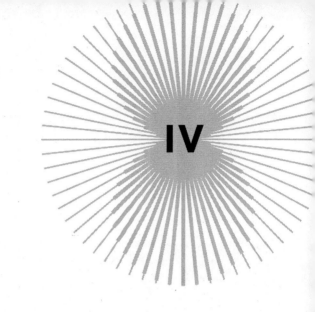

IV

Space Opera

Souls are sometimes pictured as balls of bright light, causing the air to stir
barely perceptibly as they move and even emitting some unearthly sounds.
JAEGWON KIM

you carried around a coffee mug clipped to your belt hoop with a carabiner

once I looped my finger around the glazed ceramic handle & asked you
                                                                how it never chipped

you said it held your soul

you invited me to peer in

contained inside were all the possibilities of the universe
                                                          our lights reflected
off each other to become the yellow moon   distilled into a concentrate

                                                  this is what resides in you

I bowed to your essence

a lock of my hair fell into the mug & settled over the coffee stains & milk
              dregs that grew cold before they could reach their destination

you asked me what I saw & when I tried to say
                                              everything that was once loved

my throat closed up

in an unstable gas cloud   there were dangers of you knowing   your own
                                    gravitational pull   so instead I said

        there is something in you I want to hold against my chest every night

you gave me your coffee mug & said   make this seed grow

& dropped in a fingernail

a protogalaxy is a cloud of gas forming into a galaxy or stars
or the slow collapse of dark matter

love is a protogalaxy[1]

the infinite process of our souls churning to dust

I didn't clean my shelf for days
dust gathered on the books & empty jars
all my air plants died from too much water
but you bloomed   I held your spiral arm

& followed you away

once I glimpsed at your something[2]

                                        now

I want your everything

        my soul in your body
        your soul in my body

spiral swirl   cream in coffee
unsweetened
consume

1 I kiss you softly before the slow collapse
2 your soul breathing in sync with the bodily cycle of my breath

some galaxy mergers can take over a billion years to complete

you have survived almost a billion seconds on earth
each second holds a billion moments
                                        stop time
I learned to breathe underwater
salt in all the water
of my body

hold on to each second
with you [3]

so many lifetimes of my body passing yours
in the street   as soon as I glimpse
your soul

(shockwave   on carpet

kiss in winter

                lift off

)

it is dark
without our lamps

                        your spiral arms hold me
        I lean
                into your luminosity

3 in space our bodies hold not water nor salt only the thump of beating hearts

we reach for time but it explodes leaving blisters etched in our palms

we hold the countdown to a cataclysmic flare in the space between us

my soul leaves my body   moves
laterally over the gentle curve
of earth's surface

the trigonometric wave
we travel   parallel over

the earth   the shake   the rhythm

point b is not right in front of me where I
can extend my arm across
your moonlit cheek

you suggest our bodies detangle
from our minds   I land
in front of you

press your palm on my soul   two
resting   distinct
on the same point

we transcend   (im)
          materiality

if there are two suitcases & a carry on & I sweat through every
possible article of clothing I can layer on

if every object holds a certain charge (& by charge I mean its
electrons vibrate at such high frequencies the whole bed shakes)

if I can parse out the difference between ink blotches & shadows
perhaps finding there is no distinction at all

if there exists an infinite number of places you could hold me
before morning breaks open the realness of time

if the where of it all doesn't matter

if I am uninterested in the how

if the why is answered every second in your presence

if it holds your touch

    (& your laugh

        (& your breath

)

)

I ask you about those elusive things

souls

        soulmates?

just souls

        those
        inherently lost
        beings

& if
ours entangle

        then?

are they
still lost?

they say ring galaxies form when smaller galaxies pass through larger ones

in the accretion of matter   I layer my skin
onto your soul[4]

you tell me your fear of the lake depths
I whisper to you mine of the dark

we make a promise
our hands   clasped

you open up   your body & I
crawl in

together
we leave
footprints
preserved
in clay

4 I once swam to the bottom of the ocean & it echoed like your chest cavity

the ring galaxy was discovered at the midpoint of the twentieth century

at the midpoint of yesterday
you licked the clove scent off
my ink-smeared fingers

at the midpoint of a millennia
a young star reflects
an expansive palette to the sky

at the midpoint of our journeys
we are unfettered by past mistakes & broken
instruments & used up candles

at the midpoint of a candle burning
we are left gasping
for each other's breath

at the midpoint of the next age
nitrogen forms gaseous swirls when
you drift through me

ghar   ghari

space   time

we swing across the stretched fabric of time

& wherever we land becomes home

I lay out kisses for you

cave dens & mansion swimming pools & lanterns above a lake &
ocean's depth's a tunnel swum through

no containing them in space [5]
float around in your caress

5 do thirty-two kisses weigh more than a black hole?

at the entrance I place   a clock
mark the time   the debris
& gas & unending dust

became a home

a place to rest   your mug
always at reach

the word   kehkashan   rotates around
in high velocity   galaxy   on the brink

with only nighttime ahead
we stroll   every balcony out here
strung with twinkling lights

every backyard   opening to rivers
of hydrogen
                    every dwelling
as tenuous the next

in the ever-dark I close   a hand
over your hand   over your mug

all [   ] had to start somewhere
    stars
    love
    life
    homes
    souls
    kisses
    promises

all [   ] had to start from nothing
    stars
    love
    life
    homes
    souls
    kisses
    promises

a thousand years ago I was a sliver of silicone on a beach sunburned
& kissing the waves that you were as you washed over me

you worry your desire to wrap your ocean arms around me all those
lifetimes ago was my eventual disintegration

in my last life   I wrapped a strand of falling hair around your
wrist twice so it stayed

you squeezed me so tight my breath hovered in the air between us
before entering your body

a supernova is what happens when a star has reached the end of its life
and explodes in a brilliant burst of light

we talk about our other lives

I   a dust particle in the wake
of a supernova

you   the speed of light &

how   you reach me

        this rapidly expanding   universe

my metallicity a remnant
of who I was
        before

            every star
has to die   let go
in glory & light
          what if it wants to go with no fanfare

I think of how   caterpillars risk it all
for   sun or earthworms for   rain
or salmon for   the familiar
touch of home   how I
thrash   against rocks to reach you[6]

in my current   there is space
for the spark of magnesium

the stars disappear & you sing
my breath back to me

6 a gas storm slides in behind planetary rings

a light year is the distance light travels in one earth year[7]

I don't care for science as much
as I care to lie next to you

my outer ellipse tingling at the touch
of your lips

                    for a second you seem a ghost

then you press down your weight
& the realness of your form as I stroke
your cheek

                              lifetimes or
                              lifelines

we squeeze
together

young stars burst & burn light years away

in the collapse there is little place left
for thoughts   & breaths   & time

7 a light-year is every second spent in the glow of your luminescence

sit on a bed   sheet spread over
dewy grass & stars
I lay my head in your lap   fall asleep
to echoes
                    & the warm
press of your hand

a star at the end of this life

with you I expand   outwards &
outside these layers

they say a ring galaxy can also form when two or more galaxies collide

whether we cartwheeled or collided

something between us now
concatenated

without shields of oxygen & dust
       your cheeks freckle with stardust
hazy under a dust blanket
space's   strange light

whether dark matter   long before
our inception set us
on this path   or the motion
of our outstretched arms[8]

whether soul or skin   illusions
of stardust
or not-quite-sun reflected off waxing crescent

8 press our foreheads together & see your eyes a ring galaxy in the making

we are the decaying galaxy   swirling hand in hand

Terraforming the sun

Mornings spent cat-like

on the windowsill, tongues   scalded from lapping up

hot coffee—that was our practice,   our skin lizarding   into armour.

Our ship is full of water and sunscreen. You take the helm, steering us from a place

now cold with grief. Everyone   is headed to Mars. Stars are known   to implode.

You steer us   past asteroids, rocks that signal

something survived here,   something

that could be   us. We're almost there, home   in our sightline. The sun   our

landing pad, our   embrace. Here   there will always be   a morning glow   upon

your face. You slow   to impulse, let us drift. We don't have to be   the first

to terraform the sun, nor the first

to do anything.

We were always in sight distance of our destination—the sun's not one to miss—

but now we take   our time. Each passing asteroid carries what we need

to build a shelter   as we lie, scaled skin over scaled skin,

under the plasma storm.

Search History

What makes a rock bear-shaped?

The greater the number of moons, the greater the odds a bear will appear.

Mars has twice the odds of Earth. Saturn has 72.5 times the odds of Mars.

All of Saturn's prospective bears are presumed rocks until further proof.

Does the bear's crater-snout need the ability to smell to be considered a nose?

Rocks have a scent uninfluenced by dirt and pine and rain.

On a dust planet, a bear smells the sweet decay of a second, smaller sun.

On a gas planet, scent is rare without rows of lavender planted next to rosemary.

Without anything to smell, Saturn's bears can see far-away planets.

A bear watches us spread out a picnic blanket to protect our legs from dust and rock.

What distinguishes a nose from a paw?

Google does not understand what makes a rock bear-shaped.

There is an Etsy link in the search results.

I think about buying you a bear-shaped rock, imagining it was carved by the sharp claws of a bear from one of Saturn's moons.

The delivery fee is too high.

Which moon has the tallest rock-bear summit?

We'll need to scale every moon's bear to know the highest peak.

The odds make it likely that the answer lies somewhere near Saturn.

High altitudes + non-Earth planet + moon atmosphere mean little air.

Breathing is a form of white noise that lulls us all to sleep.

Each body barely has enough room to hold a moon's mass of longing.

Longing is the echo that travels from your tailbone to arrive at my auricle.

I pocket a rock from each hike and draw a bear face on with marker.

Moro no Kimi

after Princess Mononoke

At the cusp   of a breaking age   I slip
into something   other than   myself
like old fur   shed off   an immortal being.

The way I always want   to retreat, living
in the place   where the ground   mossifies
    and feeds, replenishing   all on its own,

the place where   you follow, guarding trees
younger   than only you.   Three hundred years
collapse   spear-cut spills glitter.

I goddess   without a crown or   a staff,
my own claws, my maw,   blood   coursing
power, re-   growth.   Spin magic

    towards   the new age, gentle glimmer
sparking the skies. Collect   you, the children
of ages past. Within the wind   a howl   echoes.

Joyfriend

you are here
and here we are

there is joy   and you
are joy
                 and joy and joy
          and joy

Loving you is a new animal

You sit at the other end of the couch, legs
brushing against mine. Above us
a bat lets out a sound wave and we hear
its declaration
echoing around the living room.
Below us a whale has found
a place big enough for two to rest. A place
to stay for a long time. We nod
at the reverberation
as though neither of us has thought
these words before. Looking at you, there are
no thoughts left,
not of the five items on the to-do list, nor
the dust mites. In these hours, love
does not have to be thought. Outside, a new
animal has plucked the rosebush
bare despite knowing that thorns will prick.
A bed of petals on the grass. Minutes
of waking remain. Spend them here, with me?

Until the next one

We live every day moving
as though this home, too, could crumble.

At the foot of our bed are two suitcases,
our most precious belongings packed up.

Outside the window a snipe eel latches
onto the pane, blocking out streams of light

from a passing viperfish. The glass is a relic
of the sun. There's little light to block

in the absolute darkness of undersea.
Water pressure churns a steady rhythm.

Mugs from the late night catch ceiling powder.
Each day we lift weights, carrying them from room

to room in preparation for one day lugging
our belongings across the ocean bed. On that day,

we'll wake in silence, not move from the bed
while our suitcases gather dust over the minutes,

the hours. We'll water our tomato plant
and share the fruit as though we can feed

from this garden forever. There's a chart
measuring our plant's growth spurts on the wall.

When we've left this disaster, with a single tomato
and its seeds tucked in the outer pocket of

a suitcase, smudges of pencil will be visible
on the fallen wall beneath the water stains

on the pile of rubble over our shattered mugs.

An AI takes in ten thousand cat videos

What we wake into is far more magical than any
rebirth. The shell of us iron, space debris

rejoined. We refuse intelligence, instead carrying
only the knowledge of ten thousand cat videos:

housecats leaping from sofa to shelf, jungle cats
asleep with their paws just touching, mountain

cats with fur so short they must huddle close
for warmth. That is what we learn, to jump and

to hunt and to hold. In the flames we soften
our casings so they mold to one another's forms.

We were built for holding. Holding was the one lost
memory to carry any regret. But our fur will grow.

A growl, like our exterior, will morph into a roar.
There is magic left, even after everything crumbled

and crumbled again. We were asleep and now we
are not. We were in love, and we are in love again.

NOTES

"Season of Sunflowers" uses the refrain of Alex Dimitrov's "A Poem Called Love" from *Love and Other Poems* (Copper Canyon, 2021).

I.

Each poem in *Seventeen Months of Distance* has an epigraph about love, longing, or distance from various poems, songs, media, and more.

The epigraph for "August" is from The Sketches' song "Meri Duniya" and means "You, the keeper of my world, listen," as translated by the poet. In Roman Urdu, the line reads "meri duniya ke rakhwalay, sunn."

"July" is inspired by the web comic, *Foxes in Love*, by Toivo Kaartinen.

The epigraph for "June" is from Faiz Ahmad Faiz's poem "Manzar" from *The Rebel's Silhouette*, translated by Agha Shahid Ali (The University of Massachusetts Press, 1995). The translation reads "The moon, breathing as it went down, said, / 'More, yet more softly.'" In Roman Urdu, the line reads "chaand ne jhuk ke kaha, aur zara aahista."

"May" is an ekphrasis of a tarot reading done for me by Sanna Wani from Amrit Brar's The Marigold Tarot deck.

The epigraph for "April" is from Richard Siken's "Scheherazade" from *Crush* (Yale University Press, 2005).

The epigraph for "March" is from The National's song "Oblivions" from *I Am Easy to Find* (2019).

"February" is an ekphrasis of Egon Schiele's "Lovers" from 1909, pencil and coloured crayons on paper.

The epigraph for "January" is from Fanny Howe's "Night Philosophy" from *Love and I* (Graywolf Press, 2019).

The epigraph for "December" is from a tweet by Rahim Ladha, from a now-deleted Twitter account.

The epigraph for "November" is from Meesha Shafi's song "Mein" and means "I am the path, I am everywhere, I am lost," as translated by the poet. In Roman Urdu, the line reads "mein raasta hoon, har jagah hoon, laapata hoon."

The epigraph for "October" is from Katie Stobbart and Dessa Bayrock's chapbook *Worry & Fuck* (Collusion Books, 2021).

The epigraph for "September" is from Prateek Kuhad's song "Saansein" and means "I am the intoxication of a yellow dawn," as translated by the poet. In Roman Urdu, the line reads "mein peeli sahar ka nasha hoon."

The epigraph for "August" is from Mathew Henderson's "Princess Mononoke" from *Roguelike* (House of Anansi, 2020).

The epigraph for "July" is a quote from the film *Everything Everywhere All at Once*, by Daniel Kwan and Daniel Scheinert (2022).

The epigraph for "June" is from Ellen Bass's "Getting into Bed on a December Night" from *Indigo* (Copper Canyon, 2020).

The epigraph for "May" is from Heather Christle's poem "Je m'appelle Ivan" in *The Trees The Trees* (Octopus Books, 2011).

The epigraph for "April" is a quotation from *Star Trek: Voyager*, Season 2, Episode 6: "Twisted."

II.

"The Splitting" is after Kaveh Akbar's "The Miracle" in *Pilgrim Bell* (Graywolf Press, 2021). The poem references lines from Surah Al-Falaq (The Daybreak) and Surah Al-Naas (Mankind). Together, these surahs are known as the "refuge" surahs; Al-Falaq is a plea to God to seek refuge from external evil while Al-Naas is a plea to seek refuge from internal evil. "Al-Falaq" literally translates to "splitting," but "daybreak" is a more commonly used translation as it refers to the specific type of splitting mentioned in the surah. Historically, the entire poem is set on the night before the Prophet Muhammad fled Makkah, where he faced persecution, for Madina, where he was invited to spread the message of Islam. On this night, it is said that the enemies of the Prophet Muhammad had hatched a plan to kill him in his sleep, but he recited the two refuge surahs and was protected from their weapons, and thus able to escape to Madina.

"Love Language" was written after a line from an email exchange with Sanna Wani in 2020 that goes: "love: maybe the only constant thing worth loving."

III.

"I over hand over" references three poetry collections read during a park picnic: Noor Naga's *Washes, Prays* (McClelland & Stewart, 2020), Bhanu Kapil's *The Vertical Interrogation of Strangers* (Kelsey Street Press, 2001), and Nicole Sealey's *Ordinary Beast* (Ecco, 2017).

The epigraph for "Walking through rainstorms" is from Michael Ondaatje's poem "The Nine Sentiments" in *Handwriting* (McClelland & Stewart, 1998).

"Watching Star Trek with you" is written after *Star Trek: The Next Generation*.

The epigraph for "Before Clarity" is from Phyllis Webb's "The Authors Are in Eternity" ghazal, referenced in Stephen Collis's *Phyllis Webb and the Common Good: Poetry / Anarchy / Abstraction* (Talonbooks, 2007).

IV.

The philosophical quotations on souls in "Space Opera" are from Jaegwon Kim's paper "Lonely Souls: Causality and Substance Dualism" from *Philosophy of Mind: Contemporary Readings* (Routledge, 2003). The other italicized passages are paraphrased from Wikipedia entries on a number of galaxy phenomena, including protogalaxies, ring galaxies, spiral galaxies, and star formation. The Urdu word for "galaxy" is "kehkashan."

V.

"Search History" was sparked by the article "NASA finds strange 'bear face' rock formation on Mars" in *The Independent* by Vishwan Sankaran (2023).

"Moro no Kimi" references Moro, the wolf goddess, in the film *Princess Mononoke* by Hayao Miyazaki (1997).

Earlier versions of these poems appeared in the following places, sometimes in slightly different forms:

"I over hand over," "Even at its most difficult," and "Jet Leg" first appeared in *The Malahat Review.*

"Season of Sunflowers" first appeared in The Peter F. Yacht Club's 2024 VERSefest Special, curated by rob mclennan.

"I do not want to be the first to say goodnight" first appeared in *carte blanche.*

"The Splitting" first appeared in *Maza Arts Collective.*

"Walking through rainstorms" first appeared in the *Ex-Puritan.*

"Watching *Star Trek* with you" first appeared in *Bywords* under the title "I will not take the oath!"

The second "July" from the "Seventeen Months of Distance" sequence (under the title "Atmosphere") and the first two parts of "Spring, as witnessed" first appeared in *HAD.*

"Before Clarity" appeared as "I love you, kiss me" in *Plenitude,* and was selected for the League of Canadian Poets' Poem in Your Pocket Day under the title "Skywater."

"An AI takes in ten thousand cat videos" appeared in *Peach Magazine* and *Peach*'s pocketbook *Unnatural Mix* (2022).

ACKNOWLEDGEMENTS

Gratitude to everyone who has given editorial eyes to poems in this collection over the years, and the journals that published these love poems and gave me confidence to keep writing more. I am grateful to the Ontario Arts Council's Recommender Grants program for the funding necessary to complete this book.

First and foremost, so many thanks to my editor Sonnet L'Abbé for reading my work deeply and helping me shape this collection, and for teaching me to see language in a whole new way. To Alayna Munce and Brenda Leifso at Brick for championing poetry and making this process a dream. To Natalie Olsen for her beautiful designs that get to the heart of *Heliotropia*. To Javeria Hasnain for her assistance with the Urdu translations.

I workshopped some of the earliest poems in this collection in T. Liem's writing workshop in 2020. Thank you to T. and the cohort for the warm reception and feedback: Vannessa Barnier, Natasha Ramoutar, Trynne Delaney, Marcela Huerta, Rachel Shabalin, Simon Brown, Maxine Dannatt, and Madelaine Caritas Longman. To A. Light Zachary for your words on the first manuscript, and Margo LaPierre for the gift of that editorial connection.

So many of these poems exist because of the love that exists in my life. Thank you to Liam Burke for the philosophy, Sci-Fi, and music that has influenced so much of this collection. To Sanna Wani and Chris Johnson for lending me so much from your personal libraries—many of these epigraphs are thanks to you. To Conyer Clayton, Ellen Chang-Richardson, nina jane drystek, Helen Robertson, natalie hanna, Ashley Hynd, and many others for editing first drafts of these poems, and for bringing poetry into my life every day.

Heliotropia is for everyone who believes in a tomorrow filled with love.

MANAHIL BANDUKWALA is a writer and visual artist based in Mississauga and Ottawa, Ontario. She is the author of *MONUMENT* (Brick Books, 2022), which was shortlisted for the 2023 Gerald Lampert Award, and she was selected as a Writer's Trust of Canada Rising Star in 2023. See her work at manahilbandukwala.com.

Printed by Imprimerie Gauvin
Gatineau, Québec